Rank It!

NATURAL DISASTERS

JIM WESTCOTT

BLACK
RABBIT
BOOKS

Bolt is published by Black Rabbit Books
P.O. Box 3263, Mankato, Minnesota, 56002.
www.blackrabbitbooks.com
Copyright © 2018 Black Rabbit Books

Marysa Storm, editor; Michael Sellner, designer;
Omay Ayres, photo researcher

Cataloging-in-Publication Data is available at the Library of
Congress.
ISBN 978-1-68072-175-1 (library binding)
ISBN 978-1-68072-239-0 (e-book)
ISBN 978-1-68072-472-1 (paperback)

Printed in the United States at CG Book Printers,
North Mankato, Minnesota, 56003. 3/17

CONTENTS

CHAPTER 1

Extreme DESTRUCTION

The sky grows dark. The wind howls. It begins to swirl. Suddenly, the spinning air lifts a car off the ground. It spins the car into a tree.

Natural disasters can happen everywhere. Scientists can tell when some are coming. Other storms strike without warning. They cause incredible damage. See how some of the worst disasters rank.

CHAPTER 2

The **DISASTERS**

Earthquake in Haiti
January 12, 2010

In 2010, an earthquake shook the country of Haiti. Buildings crumbled. People were buried beneath the **rubble**. More than 1 million people lost their homes. About 4,000 schools were damaged or destroyed. The shaking only lasted 30 seconds.

The quake had a **magnitude** of 7.0. It's one of the strongest to hit Haiti.

Richter Scale

People use the Richter Scale to measure earthquakes' strengths.

less than **3.9**
minor

4.0 to 4.9
light

5.0 to 5.9
moderate

6.0 to 6.9
strong

7.0 to 7.9
major

8.0 and higher
great

RANK IT!

316,000
ESTIMATED DEATHS

300,000
ESTIMATED PEOPLE INJURED

30 seconds
LENGTH OF EVENT

up to **$14** billion
ESTIMATED COST OF DAMAGES

RANK IT!

230,000
ESTIMATED DEATHS

MORE THAN
125,000
ESTIMATED PEOPLE INJURED

1 day
LENGTH OF EVENT

$10 billion
ESTIMATED COST OF DAMAGES

Indian Ocean Tsunami
December 26, 2004

The day after Christmas in 2004, a tsunami struck. It hit countries around the Indian Ocean. An earthquake shook the ocean floor. The shaking caused water to move away from the beaches. It rushed back as huge waves. Some waves were more than 50 feet (15 meters) high. They drowned buildings and cars. The tsunami hit more than 10 countries. Thousands of locals died. Many **tourists** also lost their lives.

Tri-State Tornado
March 18, 1925

In the mid-1920s, a tornado formed above Missouri. It was massive. At one point, it was 1 mile (2 kilometers) wide. It reached a speed of 73 miles (117 km) per hour. The tornado traveled 219 miles (352 km), ripping through Missouri, Indiana, and Illinois. It tore down trees. It wrecked fields. **Crops** were blown away. Entire towns were destroyed.

RANK IT!

695
ESTIMATED DEATHS

13,000
ESTIMATED PEOPLE INJURED

3 hours and 30 minutes
LENGTH OF EVENT

$232 million
(in 2016 dollars)

ESTIMATED COST OF **DAMAGES**

storm
clouds

Winds at
different speeds
begin to rotate.

Step 1

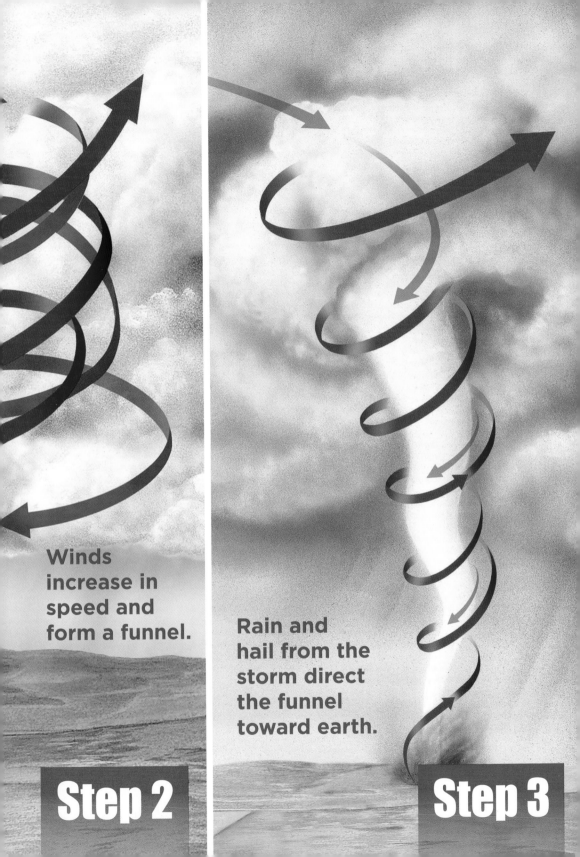

Winds increase in speed and form a funnel.

Step 2

Rain and hail from the storm direct the funnel toward earth.

Step 3

RANK IT!

1,836
ESTIMATED DEATHS

unknown
ESTIMATED PEOPLE INJURED

4 days
LENGTH OF EVENT

more than **$100** billion
ESTIMATED COST OF DAMAGES

Hurricane Katrina
August 2005

In 2005, Hurricane Katrina pounded Louisiana. It hit the city of New Orleans hard. Winds reached 175 miles (282 km) per hour. The **storm surge** was huge. The wall of water was more than 20 feet (6 m) high. The **flood walls** broke. About 80 percent of the city flooded.

Mississippi, Alabama, and parts of Florida were hit too. Towns became lakes. Katrina took many lives. It's the United States' third deadliest hurricane.

Nevado del Ruiz Eruption
November 13, 1985

In 1985, a volcano **erupted** in Colombia. At first, only ash came out. Later, **lava** poured out. It melted nearby ice, creating mudslides. Mud and rock rushed down the mountain. People in towns below were trapped. Entire homes were buried.

RANK IT! NATURAL DISASTERS

25,000 ESTIMATED DEATHS

5,000 ESTIMATED PEOPLE INJURED

1 day LENGTH OF EVENT

$1 billion ESTIMATED COST OF DAMAGES

RANK IT!

140,000
ESTIMATED DEATHS

unknown
ESTIMATED PEOPLE INJURED

2 days
LENGTH OF EVENT

$10 billion
ESTIMATED COST OF DAMAGES

Cyclone Nargis
May 2008

Most cyclones take a **predictable** path. So people thought they knew where Nargis would go. But it didn't follow the usual route. The storm went off course. It struck the Asian country Myanmar. People weren't ready for the wicked weather. Winds screamed to 135 miles (217 km) per hour. The massive storm ripped farms apart. Thousands of animals died.

The Great Appalachian Storm
November 1950

On Thanksgiving Day in 1950, a winter storm struck the eastern United States. It was huge. It was half blizzard and half hurricane. It hit 22 states. Some places got more than 50 inches (127 centimeters) of snow. Winds went faster than 100 miles (161 km) per hour. Many people lost power. Crops in the south were ruined.

353 ESTIMATED DEATHS

160 ESTIMATED PEOPLE INJURED

about 5 days LENGTH OF EVENT

$664 million (in 2016 dollars) ESTIMATED COST OF DAMAGES

European Heat Wave
June to August 2003

Heat waves can be deadly. In 2003, western Europe experienced one of the worst. It lasted months. Rivers and lakes dried up. Forest fires broke out. France had it the hardest. It was around 99 degrees Fahrenheit (37 degrees Celsius) for more than a week. Around 15,000 people in France died.

RANK IT!

35,000
ESTIMATED DEATHS

unknown
ESTIMATED PEOPLE INJURED

3 months
LENGTH OF EVENT

$14.3 billion
ESTIMATED COST OF DAMAGES

Hurricanes, cyclones, and typhoons
are all the same kind of storm. They just
form in different places.

Typhoon Usagi
September 2013

In 2013, Typhoon Usagi formed. It tore through China and nearby countries. Winds went more than 150 miles (241 km) per hour. Trees toppled. Cars went flying. Power lines and houses ripped down.

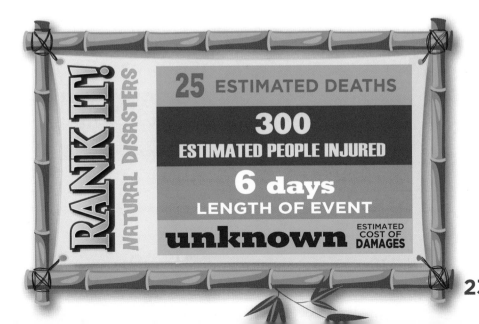

RANK IT! NATURAL DISASTERS

25 ESTIMATED DEATHS

300 ESTIMATED PEOPLE INJURED

6 days LENGTH OF EVENT

unknown ESTIMATED COST OF DAMAGES

WHERE NATURAL DISASTERS HAVE STRUCK

The Great Appalachian Storm
Canada and the United States

Hurricane Katrina
United States

Tri-State Tornado
United States

Nevado del Ruiz eruption
Colombia

Earthquake in Haiti

European Heat Wave
France, Germany, Italy, Spain, and the United Kingdom

Typhoon Usagi
China, Philippines, and Taiwan

Indian Ocean Tsunami

Cyclone Nargis
Myanmar

Great African Flood
Botswana, Mozambique, South Africa, Swaziland, and Zimbabwe

25

Great African Flood
February to March 2000

Streets became rivers. Water filled houses. In 2000, southern Africa flooded. Heavy rainfall started the flooding. And the rain just wouldn't stop. The country Mozambique was hit the hardest. It got 75 percent of its yearly rainfall in February. The flooding left people stranded. They had no clean water. They didn't have food. Crops washed away. Farms were destroyed.

RANK IT!

800
ESTIMATED DEATHS

2 months
LENGTH OF EVENT

500,000
ESTIMATED PEOPLE INJURED

$1 billion
ESTIMATED COST OF DAMAGES

CHAPTER 3

Estimated Deaths

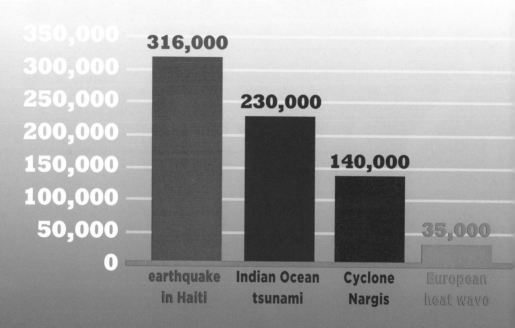

350,000
300,000
250,000
200,000
150,000
100,000
50,000
0

316,000

230,000

140,000

35,000

earthquake in Haiti   Indian Ocean tsunami   Cyclone Nargis   European heat wave

ESTIMATED COST OF DAMAGES

more than $100 billion
Hurricane Katrina

$14.3 billion
European heat wave

up to **$14 billion**
earthquake in Haiti

RANK IT!

See how they rank!

25,000	1,836	800	695	353	25
Nevada del Ruiz eruption	Hurricane Katrina	great African flood	tri-state tornado	the Great Appalachian Storm	Typhoon Usagi

ESTIMATED PEOPLE INJURED

great African flood	earthquake in Haiti	Indian Ocean tsunami
500,000	300,000	more than 125,000

Length of Event

European heat wave **3 months**

great African flood **2 months**

Typhoon Usagi **6 days**

INDEX